Homes around the world

Homes on the Water

Nicola Barber

Crabtree Publishing Company
www.crabtreebooks.com

Crabtree Publishing Company

www.crabtreebooks.com

Editors: Hayley Leach, Ellen Rodger, Michael Hodge
Senior Design Manager: Rosamund Saunders
Designer: Elaine Wilkinson
Geography consultant: Ruth Jenkins

Photo credits: Gunter Grafenhain/A1 Pix Ltd p. 8;
Roger Bamber/ Alamy p. 18; Craig Lovell/Alamy p. 20;
Vera Schimetzek/Alamy p. 13, p. 27; Hugh Sitton
Photography/Alamy p. 10, p. 26; Jim West/Alamy p. 17;
Collart Herve/Corbis Sygma p. 19; Guenter
Rossenbach/zefa/ Corbis cover, p. 7; Dennis M.
Sabangan/ epa/Corbis p. 16; Paul A Souders/Corbis p. 9;
Robert Francis/ Robert Harding World Imagery/Getty
Images p. 11; Fraser Hall/Robert Harding World
Imagery/Getty Images p. 6; Jeremy Horner/Panos
Pictures p. 23; Dermot Tatlow/Panos Pictures p. 24;
Anders Blomqvist/Lonely Planet Images 2000 p. 25; John
Elk III/Lonely Planet Images 2000 p. 15; Holger
Leue/Lonely Planet Images 2000 title page, p, 12; John
Maier Jr/Lonely Planet Images 2000 p. 21; David
Wall/Lonely Planet Images 2000 p. 22; Patrick Frilet/Rex
Features p. 14.

Cover: Brightly painted houses line a canal on the island of Burano in Venice, Italy.

Title page: In Kampong Ayer in Brunei, there are over 3,000 waterside homes on stilts. The houses are made from wood.

Activity & illustrations: Shakespeare Squared pp. 28, 29.

Because of the nature of the Internet, it is possible that some website addresses (URLs) included in this book may have changed, or sites may have changed or closed down since publication. While the author and publisher regret any inconvenience this may cause the readers, no responsibility for any such changes can be accepted by either the author or the publisher.

Library and Archives Canada Cataloguing in Publication

Barber, Nicola
    Homes on the water / Nicola Barber.

(Homes around the world)
Includes index.
ISBN 978-0-7787-3547-2 (bound).--ISBN 978-0-7787-3559-5 (pbk.)

    1. Dwellings--Juvenile literature. 2. Waterfronts--Juvenile literature.
3. Houseboats--Juvenile literature. I. Title. II. Series: Barber, Nicola.
Homes
around the world.

GT172.B37 2007   j392.3'609146   C2007-904706-8

Library of Congress Cataloging-in-Publication Data

Barber, Nicola.
    Homes on the water / Nicola Barber.
      p. cm. -- (Homes around the world)
    Includes index.
    ISBN-13: 978-0-7787-3547-2 (rlb)
    ISBN-10: 0-7787-3547-8 (rlb)
    ISBN-13: 978-0-7787-3559-5 (pb)
    ISBN-10: 0-7787-3559-1 (pb)
    1. Dwellings--Juvenile literature. 2. Waterfronts--Juvenile literature. 3.
Houseboats--Juvenile literature. I. Title. II. Series.

GT172.B37 2008
392.3'6--dc22   2007030186

Crabtree Publishing Company

www.crabtreebooks.com   1-800-387-7650

Published in Canada
Crabtree Publishing
616 Welland Ave.
St. Catharines, Ontario
L2M 5V6

Published in the United States
Crabtree Publishing
PMB16A
350 Fifth Ave., Suite 3308
New York, NY 10118

Published by CRABTREE PUBLISHING COMPANY
Copyright © **2008**

Contents

Words in **bold** can be found in the glossary on page 30

What is a waterside home?

A waterside home is a home that is located next to a river, a lake, a **canal**, or by the sea. Some waterside homes are built over the water, and some **float** on the water itself.

▼ These waterside homes are in the city of Sydney, Australia.

In some places, there are whole cities of waterside homes. The city of Venice in Italy is a waterside city. It was built on 118 small islands inside a **lagoon**. In Venice, people drive boats along the city's canals to get around the city.

Waterside life

Venice has about 150 canals crossed by around 400 bridges.

▲ These brightly painted houses line a canal on the island of Burano in Venice, Italy.

Old and new homes

In the past, people often built their homes near rivers. They used the river water for cooking, drinking, and washing. Homes were often built where people could cross easily from one side of a river to another. Sometimes, a bridge was built to cross the river.

▼ The town of Monschau, Germany, lies on the Rur river. These houses are around 300 years old.

In many towns and cities, there are big buildings called **warehouses** along rivers. The warehouses were once used for storing goods, such as food. Many warehouses have been **converted** into large **apartments** for people to live in.

▲ These warehouses in Alesund, Norway, were once used to store fish. Today, they are people's homes.

Floating homes

The Uros people live high in the Andes Mountains of South America on Lake Titicaca. They live on floating islands made out of **reeds**. The reeds grow in the lake. They build their homes out of mats made from the reeds.

▼ *This woman is sitting in front of her home on a floating island. The Uros people make boats out of reeds, too.*

Some people live in boats. This kind of boat is called a "houseboat". People cook, eat, play and sleep, and even work on their boats. Many people who live on houseboats work as fishers.

▲ *These houseboats are in Aberdeen* **harbor** *on the island of Hong Kong, China.*

11

Building a waterside home

People sometimes build their homes over the water. They push long wooden poles deep into the ground under the water to make **stilts**. In some places, people use a kind of plant called **rattan** to tie all of the different bits of wood together.

▼ In Kampong Ayer in Brunei, there are over 3,000 waterside homes on stilts. The houses are made from wood.

In the Netherlands, there are floating houses that sit on **hollow** bottoms made from **concrete**. When it rains, the houses float up as the water rises. The houses slide up and down steel poles to stop them from floating away.

Waterside life

The floating houses on the River Maas can go up and down 18 feet (5.5 meters) on their steel poles.

▲ This floating house lies on the River Maas in the Netherlands. The house has a roof made from metal.

Inside a waterside home

Houseboats are very popular in places such as Amsterdam in the Netherlands. Some houseboats are small inside, but others are big, with an upstairs and a downstairs. Old houseboats are often painted in bright colors inside and outside.

▼ *This houseboat floats on the Canal du Centre in France. It is large and comfortable inside.*

In the town of Chau Doc, Vietnam, many people live in floating homes on the Bassac River. Some of them keep fish in nets in the water underneath their homes. They feed and catch the fish by opening **trap doors** in the floors of their houses.

Waterside life

There are about 1,000 fish-farming families in Chau Doc.

▲ These two boys are feeding the fish in the nets beneath their floating home.

The weather

Floods are a danger for people who have waterside homes. If there is a lot of rain, the water in rivers can rise above the river banks and cover the land. The water will then flood homes. People often have to be rescued by boat or helicopter.

▼ *This family in the Philippines is trapped on the roof of their home by a flood. They are waiting to be rescued.*

Sometimes, storms hit towns and cities that are built by the sea. In 2005, a very strong storm called **Hurricane** Katrina hit the city of New Orleans, Louisiana. Many parts of the city were flooded after levees, or flood barriers, failed during the hurricane.

▲ *This couple is looking inside their ruined home after the floods caused by Hurricane Katrina in New Orleans, Louisiana.*

The environment

People may have to leave their seaside homes because of **erosion**. Erosion happens as the waves gradually wash away parts of the coastline. In places where the rocks are soft, the waves wash away the land more quickly than they do where the rocks are hard.

▼ *These homes on the English coast once stood far from the **cliff** edge. Waves are washing the cliff rocks away.*

In some places, living by the water is not very **healthy**. In waterside **shanty towns**, it can be difficult for people to find clean water for drinking and cooking. Using and drinking dirty water can make them sick.

▲ In this shanty town in Manaus, Brazil, the river water is dirty and full of garbage.

School and play

In some parts of the world, children go to floating schools. In Cambodia, there is a lake called Tonlé Sap. Most of the year, the lake is small. Every year, there is a time when a lot of rain falls, and the lake floods. People have floating schools and homes on this lake.

▼ These two boys are returning home from school through the waters of the Tonlé Sap in Cambodia.

Children who live in waterside homes often love to play games together in the water. They learn to swim, sail boats, dive, and fish.

Waterside life
When the Tonlé Sap floods, it spreads to five times its normal size.

▲ Children in Recife, Brazil, enjoy cooling off in the water near their homes.

Going to work

People who have waterside homes often go to work on the water. Fishers catch fish in nets or with fishing lines. The town of Ganvié in Benin is a fishing town. It is built on stilts in Lake Nokwe. The fishers use small boats called **canoes**.

▼ These women are paddling their canoes to a market in Ganvié, Benin. There, they will sell the fish that the men caught.

Many people like to go on vacation at beautiful waterside places. People who live on the coast or near lakes often work in stores, hotels, or restaurants that are visited by **tourists**. In Thailand, tourists go to visit the floating market at Ratchaburi.

▲ *The floating market in Ratchaburi happens every day. People sell fresh fruit and vegetables from their boats.*

Getting around

People who live near the water use boats to travel around. In places where there are no roads, going by boat is often the only way to get from one place to another. In the Amazon rainforest, **ferries** take supplies to far-away villages.

▼ *This boat carries a doctor to a village on the Amazon River. The boat goes to the village every two months.*

In some places, bridges join waterside **settlements**. Some bridges carry cars and other **vehicles**. Others carry trains.

Waterside life

The Öresund Link has two **decks**. Trains run on the lower deck, and there is a road on the upper deck.

▲ *This bridge joins Malmö, Sweden, with Copenhagen, Denmark.*
It is called the Öresund Link.

Where in the world?

Some of the places mentioned in this book have been labeled here. ▼

Look at these two pictures carefully.

- How are the homes different from each other?

- What is each home made from?

- Look at their walls, roofs, windows, and doors.

- How are these homes different from where you live?

- How are they the same?

NORTH AMERICA

New Orleans

ATLANTIC OCEAN

Manaus
Amazon

PACIFIC OCEAN

SOUTH AMERICA

Lake Titicaca, South America

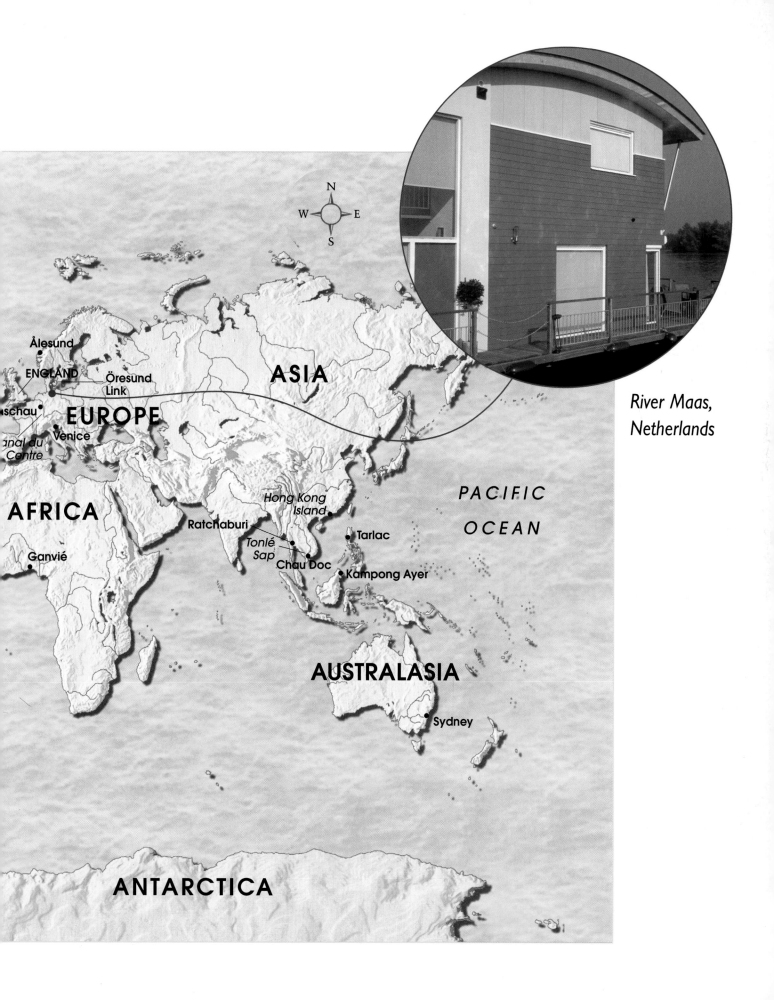

N
W ⊕ E
S

ENGLAND
Ålesund
Öresund
Link
ASIA
...schau
EUROPE
...nal du
Centre
Venice

AFRICA

Hong Kong
Island
Ratchaburi
Tonlé
Sap
Chau Doc
PACIFIC
OCEAN
Tarlac
Ganvié
Kampong Ayer

AUSTRALASIA

Sydney

ANTARCTICA

*River Maas,
Netherlands*

My own floating home

Here is an activity that allows you to see which material floats the best.

What you need
- large bowl
- glue
- paper
- water
- pebbles
- pencil
- household items (aluminum foil and paper)
- natural items (leaves and sticks)

I. Take two sheets of aluminum foil, and lay them on top of one another in a crisscross fashion. Make an open box by folding up the sides of the foil and pinching together four corners. Try to make sure that there are no spaces or openings between the sides of the foil box. Now repeat this step with two sheets of paper. You may use glue to hold the pieces of paper together and help you form the four corners.

2. Fill the bowl halfway with water. Place your aluminum foil "raft" on top of the water. Slowly place pebbles on the raft. See how many pebbles you can add before the raft sinks. Repeat this step with the paper raft. Write down the number of pebbles that you added to each raft.

3. Now try the same experiment with the natural items. Lay the sticks down side-by-side, and then glue them together. You will need to glue at least two layers of sticks together. Glue a layer of leaves on top of the sticks.

4. Place the raft on top of the water in the bowl. Begin to place pebbles on the raft. Write down the number of pebbles that the raft held without sinking.

Questions to Think About:

Which raft held the most pebbles? Which raft sank the fastest? Why do you think that this happened? As you know, it is very important to choose the right materials when building a floating home. What materials would you choose?

Glossary

apartment	A set of rooms to live in, usually on one floor of a building
canal	A human-made channel of water
canoe	A small boat that is pushed along by paddles
cliff	A steep, high rock face
concrete	A mixture of cement, sand, and water that gets harder as it dries
convert	To change into something else
deck	The floor of a ship or bridge
erosion	Gradual wearing away; waves wear away soft rocks
ferry	A boat that carries people and vehicles from place to place
float	To be held up by water
flood	When water goes onto land that is normally dry
harbor	A safe place near land for boats to stay
healthy	When someone is fit and well
hollow	Something that has an empty space inside
hurricane	A very strong storm with high winds and rain
lagoon	An area of sea water that is separated from the sea by a strip of land
rattan	A kind of climbing palm tree
reed	A kind of plant that grows in wet or marshy places
settlement	A place where people live
shanty towns	An area of roughly built homes
stilts	Poles that are used to raise something off of the ground
trap door	A small door in a floor or ceiling
tourist	A person who is on vacation
vehicle	Any kind of transport with wheels, such as a car or a truck
warehouse	A large building that is used to store goods

Further information

Books to read

Nicola's Floating Home, from the Crabapples series
Tropical Oceans, from The Living Ocean series
Life in the Ancient Indus River Valley, from the Peoples of the Ancient World series
Life of the California Coast Nations, Nations of the Northeastern Coast, Nations of the Eastern Great Lakes, Nations of the Western Great Lakes, Nations of the Norwest Coast, Native Homes, from the Native Nations of North America series

Websites

http://www.worldlakes.org/index.asp
To find out about lakes all around the world

http://news.nationalgeographic.com/kids/
National Geographic website for children

http://www.bbc.co.uk/schools/riversandcoasts/rivers/people_river/index.shtml
http://www.bbc.co.uk/schools/riversandcoasts/coasts/people_coast/index.shtml
Find out what it is like living near a river or on the coast

Index

All of the numbers in **bold** refer to photographs.

Printed in the USA